Lerner SPORTS

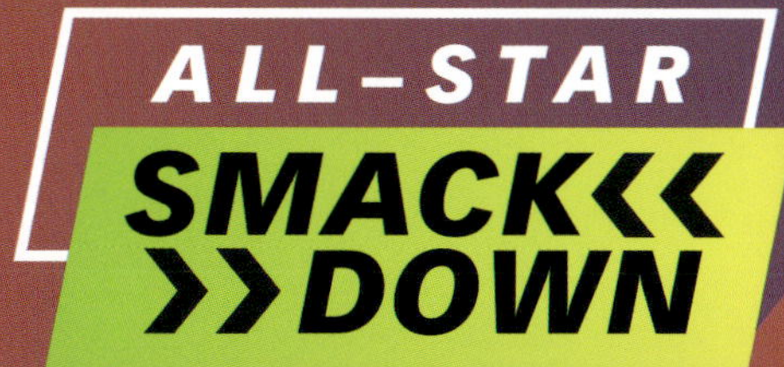

BREANNA STEWART VS. MAYA MOORE

WHO WOULD WIN?

KELLEY BARTH

Lerner Publications ◆ Minneapolis

Stats in this book are accurate through the 2024 WNBA season.

Lerner Publications Company
An imprint of Lerner Publishing Group, Inc.
241 First Avenue North
Minneapolis, MN 55401 USA

For reading levels and more information, look up this title at www.lernerbooks.com.

Main body text set in Aptifer Sans LT Pro.
Typeface provided by Linotype AG.

Library of Congress Cataloging-in-Publication Data

Names: Barth, Kelley author
Title: Breanna Stewart vs. Maya Moore : who would win? / Kelley Barth.
Other titles: Breanna Stewart versus Maya Moore
Description: Minneapolis : Lerner Publications, [2026] | Series: Lerner Sports. All-star smackdown | Includes bibliographical references and index. | Audience: Ages 7–11 | Audience: Grades 2–3 | Summary: "Breanna Stewart has won three WNBA titles and two league MVP awards. Maya Moore won four titles and one MVP award. Can you pick a winner? Read about their careers and make your choice"—Provided by publisher.
Identifiers: LCCN 2025014124 (print) | LCCN 2025014125 (ebook) | ISBN 9798765689431 lib. bdg. | ISBN 9798348028374 pbk | ISBN 9798765694268 epub
Subjects: LCSH: Women basketball players—Rating of—United States—Juvenile literature | Forwards (Basketball)—United States—Statistics—Juvenile literature | Stewart, Breanna, 1994- | Moore, Maya | Sports rivalries—United States—History—Juvenile literature | LCGFT: Statistics
Classification: LCC GV885.1 .B359 2026 (print) | LCC GV885.1 (ebook) | DDC 796.323082—dc23/eng/20250609

LC record available at https://lccn.loc.gov/2025014124
LC ebook record available at https://lccn.loc.gov/2025014125

Manufactured in the United States of America
1 – CG – 12/15/25

TABLE OF CONTENTS

Introduction
Basketball Legends 4

Chapter 1
Journey to Greatness 8

Chapter 2
Greatest Moments 14

Chapter 3
Fantastic Forwards 20

Chapter 4
And the Winner Is 24

Smackdown Breakdown. 28
Glossary. 30
Learn More 31
Index 32

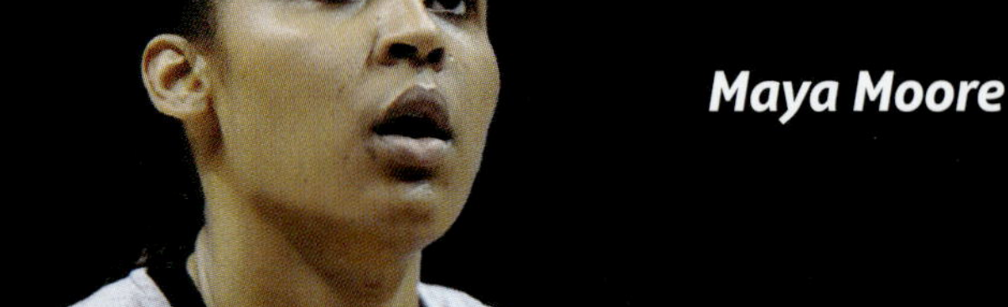

Maya Moore

INTRODUCTION

BASKETBALL LEGENDS

Maya Moore looked at the game clock. Only 1.7 seconds were left in Game 3 of the 2015 Women's National Basketball Association (WNBA) Finals. The Minnesota Lynx and the Indiana Fever were tied 77–77. The pressure was high.

FAST FACTS

- Maya Moore won four WNBA championships with the Minnesota Lynx.
- Moore is a three-time WNBA All-Star game Most Valuable Player (MVP).
- Breanna Stewart won the Final Four's Most Outstanding Player award four years in a row in college.
- Stewart is a two-time WNBA MVP and a two-time WNBA Finals MVP.

Moore was having a good game. She had 21 points and seven rebounds. But now the title was on the line. She had to help her team score quickly.

Moore received a pass from her teammate. She moved left. She dribbled right. Moore jumped to take an open shot from behind the three-point line. She sank the basket right as the buzzer sounded to end the game. The Lynx got a big win. People couldn't stop talking about Moore's game-winning shot. After two more games, the Lynx won the championship.

Nine years later, in 2024, the Lynx once again played in Game 3 of the WNBA Finals. But this time, Moore's former team was facing off against Breanna Stewart and the New York Liberty. Stewart was ready to make history.

Breanna Stewart

The Liberty had fallen behind, but Stewart wasn't about to give up. With 30 points, 11 rebounds, and four blocks, her effort turned the game around. In the second half, Stewart scored 13 points in a row and helped the Liberty come from behind to win the game. Two games later, the Liberty won their first title.

Moore and Stewart are two of the best forwards in basketball history. They have many championships and awards to their names. But who would win in a head-to-head matchup? Let the smackdown begin!

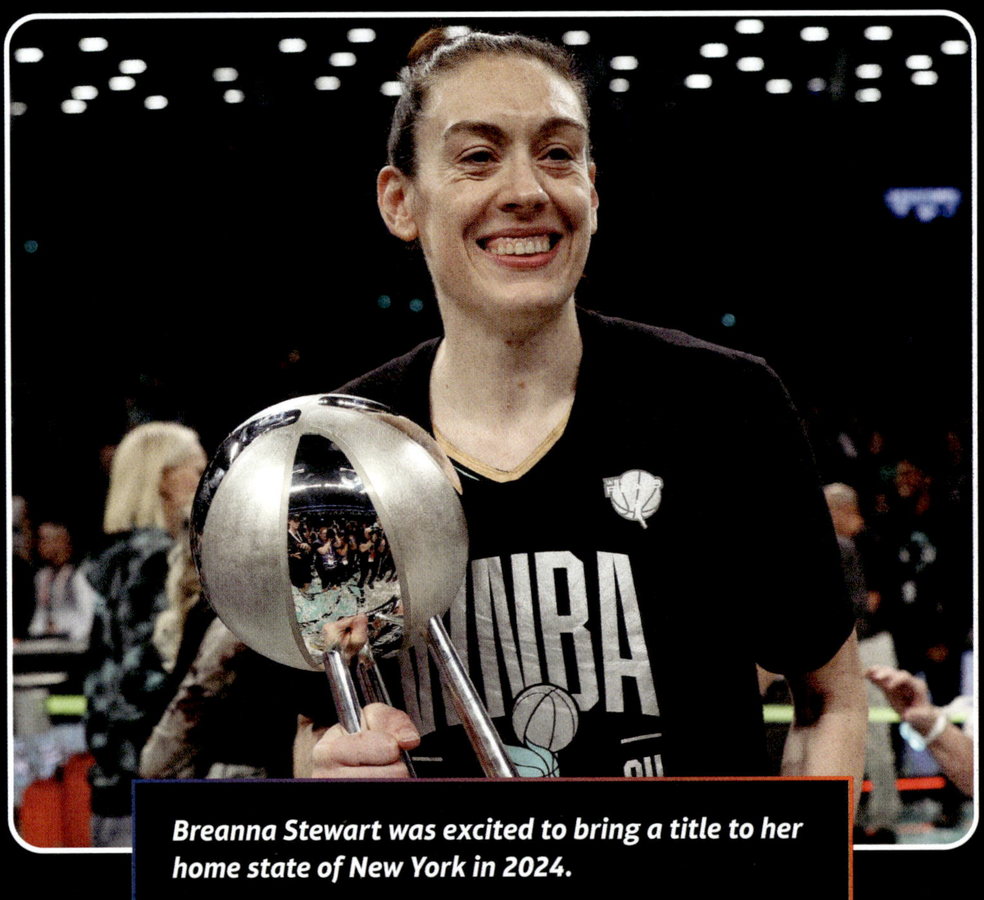

Breanna Stewart was excited to bring a title to her home state of New York in 2024.

Maya Moore is one of only seven WNBA players with four championship wins. She shares the record with Sue Bird, Seimone Augustus, Sheryl Swoopes, Tina Thompson, Rebekkah Brunson, and Cynthia Cooper.

CHAPTER 1

Moore competes at the McDonald's All American Games in 2007.

JOURNEY TO GREATNESS

Maya Moore was born on June 11, 1989, in Jefferson City, Missouri. She started playing basketball when her mom hung a toy hoop on the back of their apartment door. As Maya grew up, she kept practicing. People soon noticed her talent on the court.

In high school in Georgia, Moore won many championships and national awards. College coaches took notice. In 2007, Moore agreed to play for the University of Connecticut

(UConn) Huskies. UConn is one of women's college basketball's top teams.

Moore got off to a strong start in college. In her first year, she scored more points than any other freshman in UConn history. In 2009, Moore helped lead her team to the national championship. They won the title again the following year. Moore was a star. She remains the only player in UConn history to score more than 3,000 points in a career.

Moore runs down the court during the 2011 Final Four.

Moore led the Huskies to 150 wins. They only lost four games during her four years at UConn. It was no surprise that the Minnesota Lynx picked Moore first overall in the 2011 WNBA Draft.

Breanna Stewart was born on August 27, 1994, in North Syracuse, New York. She also showed an early talent for basketball. Breanna was a tall girl. She developed her basketball skills as she dribbled a ball around her neighborhood.

Her practice paid off. Like Moore, Stewart won multiple basketball awards in high school. Stewart's skills also earned her a spot at UConn.

Stewart goes up for a shot against Courtney Williams during the McDonald's All American Games in 2012.

Stewart smiles after making a basket during the 2016 Final Four.

While Maya Moore was making her mark on the WNBA in 2012, Stewart was a freshman for the Huskies. Stewart scored 169 points in her first 10 games at UConn. This broke the school record that Moore had set five years earlier. But Stewart didn't stop there.

Stewart helped lead the team to four straight national championships. Even on a great team, she stood out. Stewart was named the Final Four's Most Outstanding Player all four years she played. In 2016, she once again followed in Moore's footsteps. The Seattle Storm made Stewart the first overall WNBA draft pick.

Stewart celebrates her fourth college championship win in 2016.

CONSIDER THIS

Moore and Stewart aren't the only WNBA All-Stars who went to UConn. Great players such as Sue Bird, Diana Taurasi, Swin Cash, and Tina Charles also played for the Huskies.

From left to right: *Team USA members Breanna Stewart, Maya Moore, Geno Auriemma, Tina Charles, Sue Bird, and Diana Taurasi at the 2016 Olympics. Auriemma coached all five players at UConn.*

CHAPTER 2

Moore dribbles past Los Angeles Sparks player Jenna O'Hea during Moore's first WNBA season.

GREATEST MOMENTS

Maya Moore got off to a strong start in the WNBA. During her first year, she averaged 13.2 points and 1.4 steals per game. She won the league's 2011 Rookie of the Year award.

Moore also helped the Lynx make it to the 2011 WNBA Finals against the Atlanta Dream. During Game 3, Moore scored 15 points, including two three-pointers. She also had seven rebounds and two assists. She helped the Lynx win their first championship in team history.

Moore and the Lynx weren't done yet. Two years later, they won another title. Moore was the highest-scoring player in two of the three Finals games and won the Finals MVP award. The location of this win was special to Moore. The final game was held at State Farm Arena in Atlanta, Georgia. It was the same arena where she had won three Georgia state championships in high school.

Moore pumps up the crowd during the 2017 WNBA Finals.

After her amazing career ended, Maya Moore joined the Women's Basketball Hall of Fame in 2024.

In 2014, Moore won the WNBA MVP award. But she wasn't done winning championships. In 2015 and 2017, Moore helped her team win two more WNBA titles. In 2017, Moore scored 18 points and had 10 rebounds in Game 5 to help the Lynx win their fourth championship in seven years. There was no doubt that she would go down in history as one of the league's best players.

Breanna Stewart also got off to a strong start in the WNBA. She scored 23 points for the Seattle Storm in her first WNBA game. That year, she won the 2016 Rookie of the Year award.

CONSIDER THIS

Both Moore and Stewart are known for putting big numbers up on the scoreboard. In 2014, Moore led the WNBA with an average of 23.9 points per game. In 2022, Stewart took the honor with 21.8 points per game.

In the 2018 season, Stewart continued to score high numbers. She made more than half of the shots she took and won the WNBA MVP award. Stewart helped the Storm make it to the WNBA Finals that season. In the last game, Stewart had 30 points, eight rebounds, and three assists. She won the Finals MVP award, and the Storm won their first championship in eight years.

Stewart dribbles down the court during a 2017 game against the Los Angeles Sparks.

Stewart missed the 2019 season because of an ankle injury. But that didn't slow her down when she returned in 2020. Stewart and the Storm won another championship that season. Stewart was the top scorer in all three games of the WNBA Finals. Once again, she won the Finals MVP award.

In 2023, Stewart joined the New York Liberty. The Liberty had never won a WNBA title. No New York pro basketball team had won a championship since 1976. Stewart grew up in the state, and she was determined to help the Liberty end New York's losing streak.

Stewart runs toward the basket in the 2023 WNBA Finals.

Stewart (center left) defends the net against Minnesota Lynx player Napheesa Collier in the 2024 WNBA Finals.

In her first home game with the Liberty, Stewart scored 45 points. That was a team record and a career-high for Stewart. The Liberty won 32 games that season. It was their best season in team history. They made it to the WNBA Finals. Despite Stewart's fantastic rebounding, they lost in four games. Later that year, she won her second WNBA MVP award.

In 2024, the team repeated their success. Stewart led the team in points and steals. The Liberty advanced to the WNBA Finals against the Lynx. In Game 5 of the Finals, Stewart scored 13 points and had 15 rebounds. The game went into overtime, and Stewart sank two free throws to help the Liberty finally win a WNBA title. Stewart had done what she set out to do.

CHAPTER 3

Moore competes in a game against Japan at the 2016 Olympics.

FANTASTIC FORWARDS

Moore and Stewart are some of the best forwards in the game. They shine on both offense and defense. Both Moore and Stewart have played in the WNBA All-Star game six times. Moore even won the title of All-Star MVP three times.

Moore and Stewart didn't just find success in the WNBA. They are also Olympic athletes. Moore won gold medals in 2012 and 2016 with the USA Basketball Women's National

Team. Stewart has three gold medals with the team from the 2016, 2020, and 2024 Olympics.

Stewart and Moore are alike in many ways. However, there are a few differences. Moore was a better free-throw shooter.

Stewart competes at her third Olympic Games in 2024.

CONSIDER THIS

Moore and Stewart played for different WNBA teams. But in 2016, they were Olympic teammates. Together, they scored 25 points to help the United States win the gold medal match against Spain.

She also made more three-point shots. Stewart dominates on rebounds and blocks. That makes her a very successful defender. She also has had fewer turnovers than Moore did.

Moore speaks at the White House next to President Barack Obama in 2014 after the Minnesota Lynx's second championship win.

Stewart speaks at a charity event in 2019.

Moore and Stewart are superstars off the court too. Moore left the WNBA in 2018 to work on social justice issues. In 2021, she received the Arthur Ashe Courage Award for her work. Stewart has also spoken out for justice and equal rights. This work, along with her athletic skills, helped her win the 2020 *Sports Illustrated* Sportsperson of the Year award.

CHAPTER 4

Moore sprints down the court in a 2018 game against the Los Angeles Sparks.

AND THE WINNER IS

Who wins this all-star smackdown? It is a tight matchup. Many people will have different opinions. Think about each player's big wins and awards. Consider their stats. Decide for yourself who the winner should be.

Both players have proven their talent. Moore played all 271

of her WNBA games with the Minnesota Lynx. She helped the Lynx win four titles. Stewart has helped win titles for two different teams. In 2024, she led the New York Liberty to their first title. While Moore has more championships, Stewart is a two-time MVP both in the regular season and in the WNBA Finals. Moore won each of those MVP awards once.

Stewart celebrates the Liberty's championship win in 2024.

Moore and Stewart have also both been part of the All-WNBA First Team multiple times. This is a team made up of the best players in the league. Moore was on the All-WNBA First Team five times. Stewart has been on the team six times. She has also proved her strength as a defensive player. She has been on the WNBA All-Defensive First Team three times.

When comparing great players such as Stewart and Moore and choosing a winner, there is no right or wrong answer. They are both all-time great athletes. But Stewart wins this smackdown at the buzzer.

Now it's your turn. What do you think? Which all-star has what it takes to win this smackdown?

Moore prepares to shoot against the Connecticut Sun in 2014.

Stewart leads the New York Liberty to another win on June 2, 2024, in their home arena, Barclays Center.

SMACKDOWN BREAKDOWN

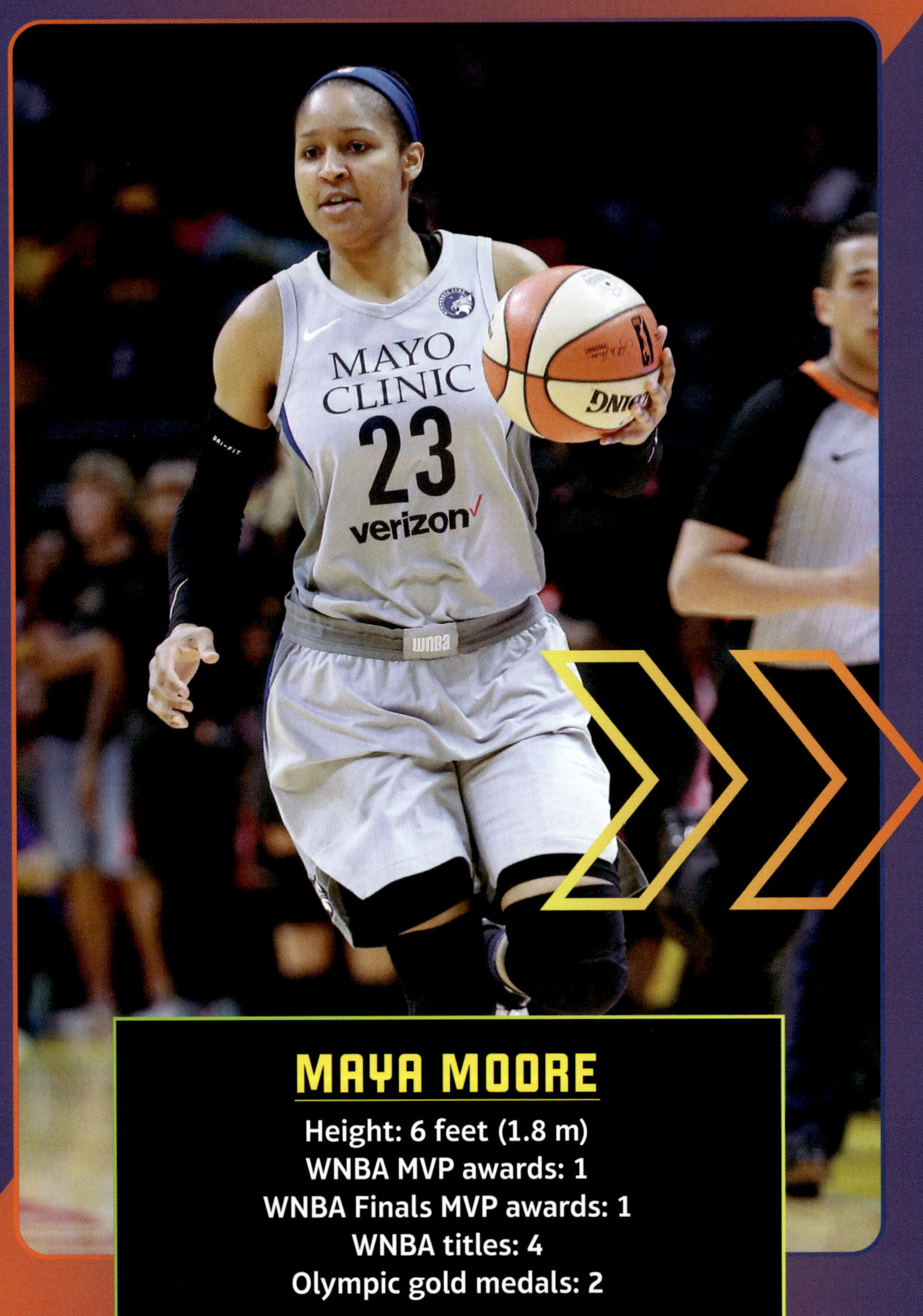

MAYA MOORE

Height: 6 feet (1.8 m)
WNBA MVP awards: 1
WNBA Finals MVP awards: 1
WNBA titles: 4
Olympic gold medals: 2

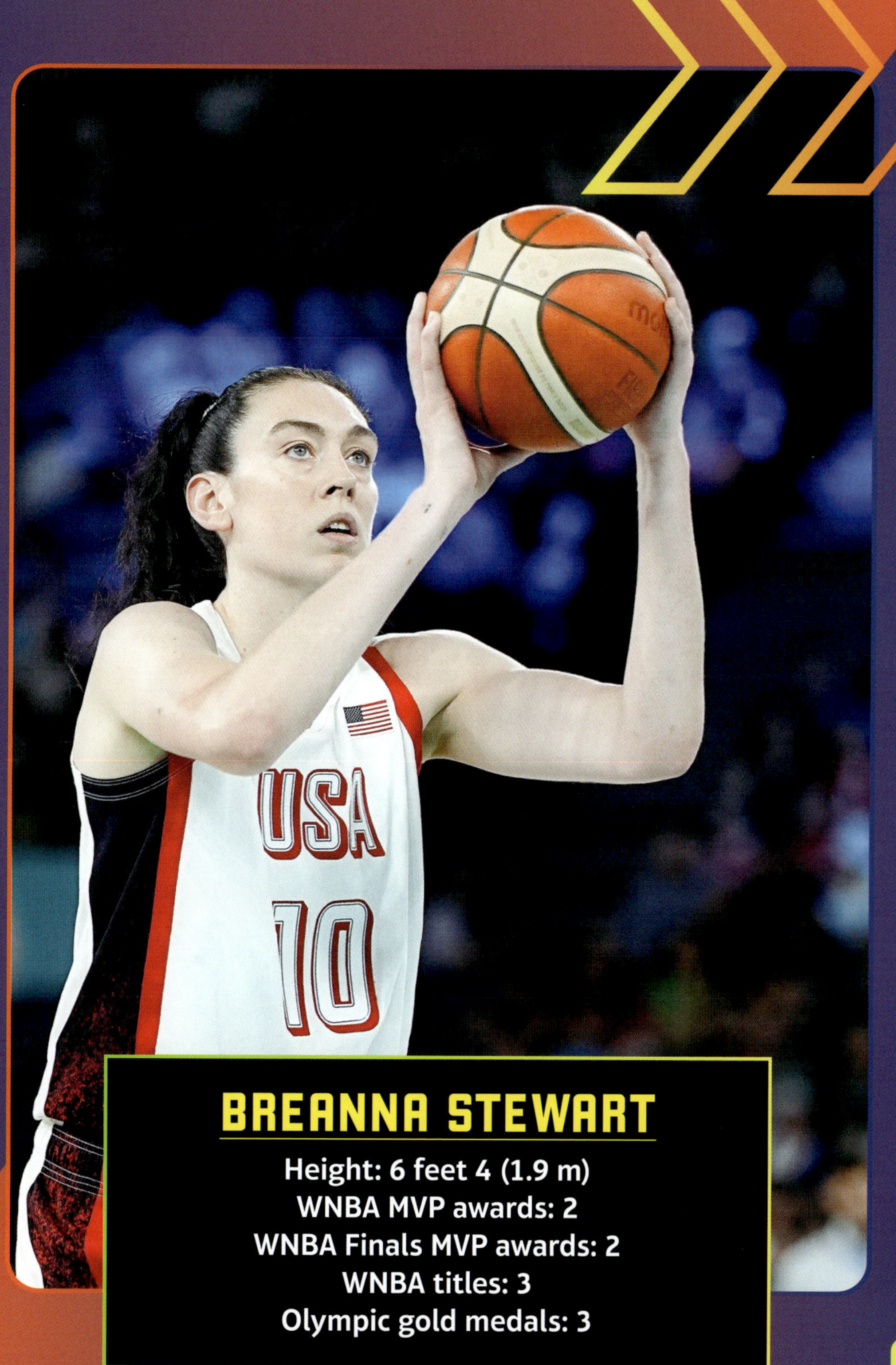

BREANNA STEWART

Height: 6 feet 4 (1.9 m)
WNBA MVP awards: 2
WNBA Finals MVP awards: 2
WNBA titles: 3
Olympic gold medals: 3

GLOSSARY

assist: a pass to a teammate that leads directly to a score

block: when the ball is knocked away by a defender before reaching the hoop

draft: when teams take turns choosing new players

Final Four: the last four teams in the national college basketball tournament

rebound: grabbing and controlling the ball after a missed shot

rookie: a player in their first year

steal: when a player takes the ball from an opposing player

title: championship

turnover: when the other team takes control of the ball after an error or a foul

LEARN MORE

Anderson, Josh. *New York Liberty*. Minneapolis: Lerner Publications, 2025.

Reeves, Diane Lindsey. *G.O.A.T. College Women's Basketball Players*. Minneapolis: Lerner Publications, 2025.

Sports Illustrated Kids—WNBA
https://www.sikids.com/tag/wnba

UCONN Women's Basketball
https://uconnhuskies.com/sports/womens-basketball

Whiting, Jim. *The Story of the Minnesota Lynx*. Mankato, MN: Creative Education and Creative Paperbacks, 2024.

Women's National Basketball Association Facts for Kids
https://kids.kiddle.co/Women%27s_National_Basketball_Association

INDEX

Arthur Ashe Courage Award, 23

Minnesota Lynx, 4–5, 10, 14–16, 19, 25
Most Valuable Player (MVP), 4, 15–20, 25

NCAA Final Four, 4, 12
New York Liberty, 5–6, 18–19, 25

Olympics, 20–22

Rookie of the Year, 14, 16

Seattle Storm, 12, 16–18
Sports Illustrated Sportsperson of the Year, 23

University of Connecticut (UConn), 8–11, 13

WNBA Finals, 4–5, 14–15, 17–19, 25

PHOTO ACKNOWLEDGMENTS

Image credits: William Paul/Icon Sportswire/Corbis/Getty Images, p. 4; Ethan Miller/Getty Images, p. 5; Elsa/Getty Images, p. 6; Leon Bennett/Getty Images, p. 7; Michale Hickey/WireImage/Getty Images, p. 8; Jamie Sabau/Getty Images, p. 9; Hyoung Chang/The Denver Post/Getty Images, p. 10; Andy Lyons/Getty Images, p. 11; Andy Lyons/Getty Images, p. 12; Tim Clayton/Corbis/Getty Images, p. 13; Jerry Holt/Star Tribune via Getty Images/Getty Images, p. 14; Hannah Foslien/Getty Images, p. 15; Hannah Foslien/Getty Images, p. 16; Leon Bennett/Getty Images, p. 17; Sarah Stier/Getty Images, p. 18; Elsa/Getty Images, p. 19; Alex Livesay/Getty Images, p. 20; Tim Clayton/Corbis/Getty Images, p. 21; MANDEL NGAN/AFP/Getty Images, p. 22; Matt Winkelmeyer/Getty Images for Cedars Sinai Sports Spectacular/Getty Images, p. 23; David Berding/Icon Sportswire/Getty Images, p. 24; Elsa/Getty Images, p. 25; Tim Clayton/Corbis/Getty Images, p. 26; Rich Graessle/Icon Sportswire/Getty Images, p. 27; Leon Bennett/Getty Images, p. 28; Daniela Porcelli/Eurasia Sport Images/Getty Images, p. 29.

Cover: Mingo Nesmith/Icon Sportswire/Newscom; Jeff Wheeler/ZUMA Press/Newscom.